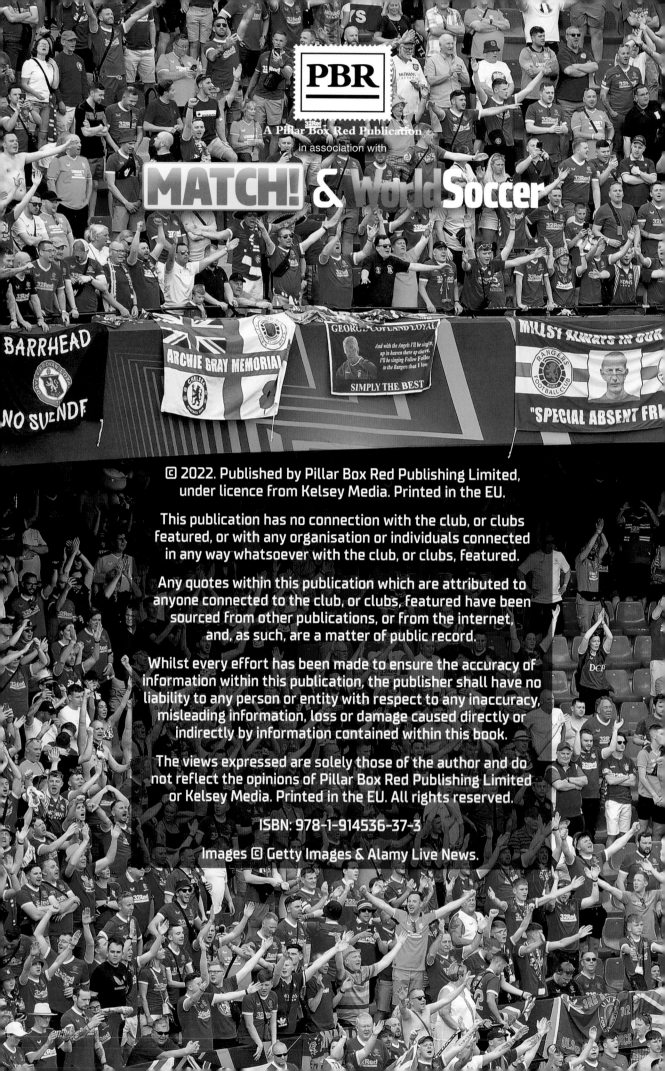

PBR

A Pillar Box Red Publication

in association with

MATCH! & WorldSoccer

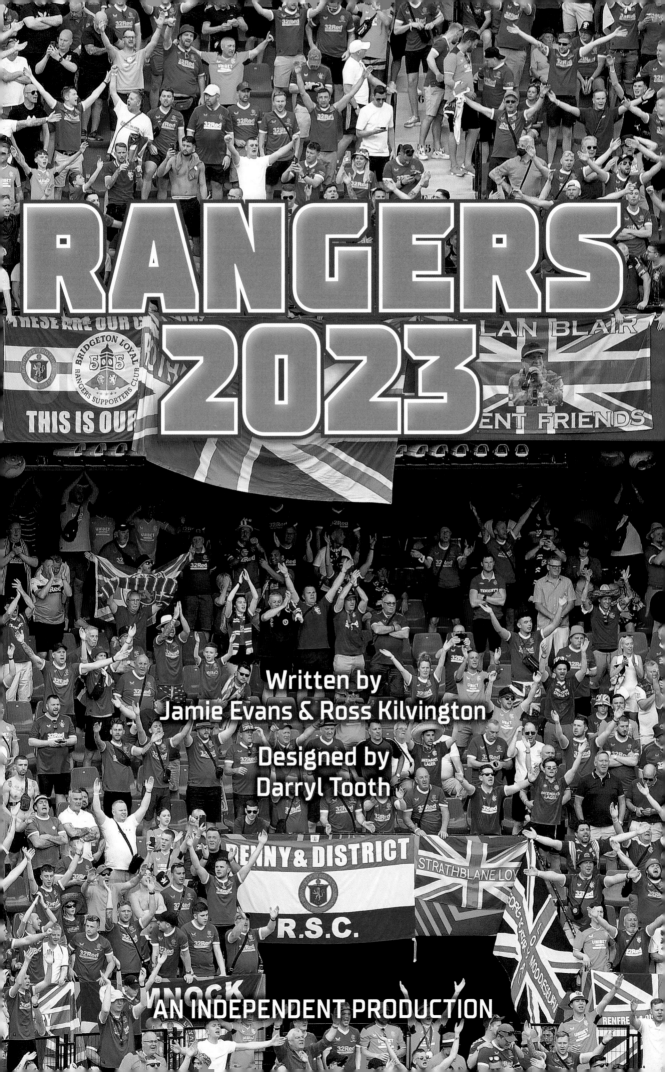

RANGERS 2023

Written by
Jamie Evans & Ross Kilvington

Designed by
Darryl Tooth

AN INDEPENDENT PRODUCTION

CONTENTS

SEASON REVIEW

We take a look back through the highs and lows of RANGERS' incredible 2021-22 season to find out the biggest moments and star performers!

JULY-AUGUST

MEGA MOMENTS!

New boy Lundstram

The Scottish Premiership season actually started on the last day of July, with Rangers blowing away Livingston 3-0 to begin the defence of their title! Steven Gerrard added four players to his squad – John Lundstram, Fashion Sakala, Nnamdi Ofoborh and Juninho Bacuna. The Gers won three of their first four league matches, including an outstanding victory over Old Firm rivals Celtic that took their unbeaten streak against them to six matches! The only setback was a shock defeat to Dundee United, although the Scottish League Cup campaign got off to the perfect start with a 5-0 win over Dunfermline!

Shock European exit

The club was expected to do well in Europe, however there was a major shock when Swedish champions Malmo defeated The Gers 4-2 on aggregate to knock them out in the Champions League qualifiers!

Europa League draw

Hopes then laid in the Europa League, and a tense 1-0 aggregate triumph over Armenian side Alashkert saw Gerrard lead his men into the group stage for the fourth consecutive season. An incredible run!

MAN OF THE MONTH!

ALFREDO MORELOS The Gers talisman picked up where he left off last season and scored three times while grabbing an assist to help the team qualify for the group stages of the Europa League!

DID YOU KNOW?

Rangers' 1-0 defeat to Dundee United in their second league game of the season was their first Scottish Premiership loss since March 4, 2020 – a jaw-dropping run of 40 matches!

RANGERS' RESULTS

31/07	PRE	Rangers	3-0	Livingston
03/08	UCL	Malmo	2-1	Rangers
07/08	PRE	Dundee United	1-0	Rangers
10/08	UCL	Rangers	1-2	Malmo
13/08	LEC	Rangers	5-0	Dunfermline
19/08	UEL	Rangers	1-0	Alashkert
22/08	PRE	Ross County	2-4	Rangers
26/08	UEL	Alashkert	0-0	Rangers
29/08	PRE	Rangers	1-0	Celtic

SEPTEMBER

MEGA MOMENTS!

Home defeat to Lyon

Gerrard was keen for his side to make a fast start in the Europa League like the previous season, but consecutive defeats to Lyon and Sparta Prague gave them a battle to qualify for the next round.

Gerrard pitchside

On the domestic front, The Gers were winning matches but doing it the hard way. A nervy 2-1 win over St. Johnstone, in which they had to come from behind to claim all three points was followed by a stuttering 1-1 draw with Motherwell, as new signing Fashion Sakala scored his first competitive goal for The Gers!

Routine wins over Livingston in the League Cup quarter-finals and then Dundee ensured the club remained on top of the table and continued their quest for more trophies, although the Euro disappointments were hard to take as the club had been excellent on the continent over the past two seasons!

Roofe in action

MAN OF THE MONTH!

KEMAR ROOFE The forward scored twice in wins v St. Johnstone and Livingston. His first season at Ibrox was hampered by injuries and these goals would give Gerrard a selection headache going forward!

DID YOU KNOW?

Fashion Sakala became the first Zambian to score for Rangers when he netted the opener v Motherwell!

RANGERS' RESULTS

Date	Comp	Home	Score	Away
11/09	PRE	St. Johnstone	1-2	Rangers
16/09	UEL	Rangers	0-2	Lyon
19/09	PRE	Rangers	1-1	Motherwell
22/09	LEC	Rangers	2-0	Livingston
25/09	PRE	Dundee	0-1	Rangers
30/09	UEL	Sparta Prague	1-0	Rangers

OCTOBER

MEGA MOMENTS!

Sakala celebrates

The Gers endured mixed results in October, with momentum falling away slightly in the Premiership. A 2-1 win over Hibs was followed by a 1-1 draw with Hearts where Allan McGregor made a last minute howler to let the Jambos score! Rangers missed Ryan Kent, who was out injured, although deadly duo Roofe and Morelos inspired a comeback win against St. Mirren! Another league draw with Aberdeen meant Rangers had dropped nine points already, with The Gers only dropping a total of 12 in the whole of last year's title-winning campaign! The month ended with a 6-1 stuffing of Motherwell, with Sakala grabbing a hat-trick!

Euro joy versus Brondby

There was progress in Europe however, with Gerrard leading his side to their first group stage victory against Brondby. Balogun and Roofe grabbed the vital goals, and it gave the side a chance to qualify for the knockout rounds.

October also brought some sad news, as Rangers legend Walter Smith passed away at the age of 73. He won an incredible 21 major honours as Rangers manager and goes down as one of the finest managers at Ibrox.

Paying tribute

MAN OF THE MONTH!

FASHION SAKALA The gong for this month goes to the Zambian forward, who became the first African player since Sone Aluko in 2012 to score a hat-trick for The Gers – an absolutely brilliant achievement!

DID YOU KNOW?

Steven Gerrard recorded his 26th win in Europe with The Gers as they defeated Brondby 2-0 – the most of any Rangers manager in history!

RANGERS' RESULTS

Date	Comp	Home	Score	Away
03/10	PRE	Rangers	2-1	Hibernian
16/10	PRE	Rangers	1-1	Hearts
21/10	UEL	Rangers	2-0	Brondby
24/10	PRE	St. Mirren	1-2	Rangers
27/10	PRE	Rangers	2-2	Aberdeen
31/10	PRE	Motherwell	1-6	Rangers

NOVEMBER

MEGA MOMENTS!

Hibs dump out Rangers

Morelos sinks Sparta Prague

The month started off with a disappointing 1–1 draw with Brondby in the Europa League, with Ianis Hagi equalising with just over ten minutes to play. That was followed by a 4–2 victory over Ross County. It turned out to be Steven Gerrard's final game in charge of The Gers as he joined Aston Villa, and even worse was to follow as Hibs sent Rangers out of the League Cup in a shock 3–1 defeat!

There was some good news however, as former Rangers superstar Giovanni van Bronckhorst was announced as the club's new manager – and he got off to a flying start, leading the side to a 2–0 win over Sparta Prague which secured a place in the knockout round play-offs! Morelos was the star man, notching a double as he looked fit and ready to get back to his goalscoring best! The Dutchman got a win in his first league match in charge too, with Joe Aribo, Scott Arfield and Sakala scoring to secure three points in a 3–1 victory over Livingston!

RANGERS' RESULTS

04/11	UEL	Brondby	1-1	Rangers
07/11	PRE	Rangers	4-2	Ross County
21/11	LEC	Rangers	1-3	Hibernian
25/11	UEL	Rangers	2-0	Sparta Prague
28/11	PRE	Livingston	1-3	Rangers

MAN OF THE MONTH!

JOE ARIBO The Nigeria international took his game to a new level in November, scoring two amazing goals and also grabbing an assist!

DID YOU KNOW?

Giovanni van Bronckhorst became just the 17th permanent manager in the club's 149-year history!

DECEMBER

MEGA MOMENTS!

Rangers were heading into the busy festive period full of confidence under the new manager. With seven important matches to get through, this was going to be an important month for The Gers! All six league matches ended in victory, with the only real wobble coming against Hibernian, where it took a penalty from Kemar Roofe to secure all three points!

Van Bronckhorst

Wrapping up the Europa League group stage with a solid 1–1 draw with Lyon meant that Rangers finished in second place in the group – and they drew German giants Borussia Dortmund in the next round. Tough draw!

Drawing with Lyon

MAN OF THE MONTH!

ALLAN MCGREGOR The veteran goalkeeper played six matches in December and kept six clean sheets, an amazing month for the Rangers legend!

DID YOU KNOW?

In Van Bronckhorst's first nine matches in charge of the club, The Gers only conceded two goals!

The victories were important but so were the clean sheets, and The Gers' defence was simply incredible in December, keeping six clean sheets out of seven matches!

Heroics from Allan McGregor

RANGERS' RESULTS

01/12	PRE	Hibernian	0-1	Rangers
04/12	PRE	Rangers	3-0	Dundee
09/12	UEL	Lyon	1-1	Rangers
12/12	PRE	Hearts	0-2	Rangers
15/12	PRE	Rangers	2-0	St. Johnstone
18/12	PRE	Rangers	1-0	Dundee United
26/12	PRE	Rangers	2-0	St. Mirren

JANUARY

MEGA MOMENTS!

Arfield netted v Livi

Due to the winter break being brought forward, The Gers' first match was against Aberdeen on January 18 and it ended in a poor 1-1 draw. Rangers struggled in the next game against Livingston, winning only 1-0 before yet another poor showing in the Highlands against Ross County. The Ibrox side were winning when Ross County scored with the last kick of the match to steal a point and reduce the side's lead at the top of the table. Unlucky!

The highlight of a bad month was the Scottish Cup win against Stirling Albion. A 4-0 stuffing, which featured four different scorers, was made even better when youngster Alex Lowry scored his first ever goal for the club in his first appearance! What a way to make an impact.

Wonderkid Alex Lowry

Loanee Ramsey

January also saw some new arrivals at Ibrox, most notably Wales superstar Aaron Ramsey and young Man. United winger Amad Diallo – both on loan until the end of the season!

RANGERS' RESULTS

18/01	PRE	Aberdeen	1-1	Rangers
21/01	FAC	Rangers	4-0	Stirling Albion
26/01	PRE	Rangers	1-0	Livingston
29/01	PRE	Ross County	3-3	Rangers

MAN OF THE MONTH!

ALEX LOWRY The 18-year-old came off the bench against Stirling Albion to score a dream debut goal and even started the next match against Livingston in the Premiership! He has a mega bright future!

DID YOU KNOW?

Aaron Ramsey became only the fourth Welsh player to sign for Rangers following his move from Juventus!

FEBRUARY

MEGA MOMENTS!

Celtic humbling

The month got off to a bad start with a 3-0 defeat to Celtic. It was Van Bronckhorst's first defeat in charge and the title race was heating up! The Gers responded well though, beating Hearts and Hibs 5-0 and 2-0, with six different players scoring! However, any momentum was soon ended as back-to-back league draws with Dundee United and Motherwell gave Celtic the advantage.

There was progress in the Scottish Cup, with an easy 3-0 win over Annan Athletic that saw Filip Helander return from injury to score the first goal!

The highlight of the month, and maybe even the season so far, was the victory over Borussia Dortmund in the Europa League. A stunning 4-2 win in Germany gave The Gers a huge boost going into the match at Ibrox. A 2-2 draw in Glasgow saw the club reach the last 16 and send the favourites spinning out of the competition. What a result!

Captain fantastic Tavernier

RANGERS' RESULTS

02/02	PRE	Celtic	3-0	Rangers
06/02	PRE	Rangers	5-0	Hearts
09/02	PRE	Rangers	2-0	Hibernian
12/02	FAC	Annan Athletic	0-3	Rangers
17/02	UEL	B. Dortmund	2-4	Rangers
20/02	PRE	Dundee United	1-1	Rangers
24/02	UEL	Rangers	2-2	B. Dortmund
27/02	PRE	Rangers	2-2	Motherwell

MAN OF THE MONTH!

JAMES TAVERNIER The right-back scored four goals and registered one assist in an impressive month. His three goals against Borussia Dortmund over the two legs were crucial in the aggregate win. He is quite simply Rangers' captain marvel!

DID YOU KNOW?

The Gers' 4-2 win against Dortmund was their first victory against a German team in Europe since 2008!

MARCH

MEGA MOMENTS!

150 years – Rangers were founded in 1872

March was a special month for the club as the 150th anniversary was celebrated! However, the performances on the pitch weren't very special as The Gers struggled in two vital 1-0 wins over St. Johnstone and Aberdeen in the league.

Red Star beaten

The Euro journey was becoming a distraction for the poor league form and Van Bronckhorst led Rangers to an excellent 3-0 win over Red Star Belgrade at Ibrox, with Tavernier, Morelos and Balogun all grabbing the goals. A 2-1 defeat in the away leg still meant the club progressed to the quarter-finals!

Cup progress

In between these matches was a 3-0 Scottish Cup win against Dundee, which set up an Old Firm semi-final in April! The last match of the month saw The Gers come from behind to score in the last five minutes in a 2-1 win against Dundee that kept the club on track for three trophies!

RANGERS' RESULTS

02/03	PRE	St. Johnstone	0-1	Rangers
05/03	PRE	Rangers	1-0	Aberdeen
10/03	UEL	Rangers	3-0	Red Star Belgrade
13/03	FAC	Dundee	0-3	Rangers
17/03	UEL	Red Star Belgrade	2-1	Rangers
20/03	PRE	Dundee	1-2	Rangers

MAN OF THE MONTH!

CONNOR GOLDSON The wicked Gers centre-back scored the late winner against Dundee in the league and starred as the club made the Europa League quarter-finals, while helping the team keep clean sheets in four of their six matches during March!

DID YOU KNOW?

The 3-0 win over Dundee meant Rangers progressed to their first Scottish Cup semi-final since 2018!

APRIL

MEGA MOMENTS!

Braga defeat

The club faced seven important matches in April, and they would have to do it without star striker Alfredo Morelos who was ruled out for the rest of the season through injury! A disappointing 2-1 defeat to Celtic meant April started off badly and that was followed by a 1-0 away defeat to Braga in the Europa League, meaning The Gers had it all to do in the second leg!

St. Mirren were stuffed 4-0 in the league, with Roofe grabbing a hat-trick, and this confidence boost inspired them to defeat Braga 3-1 after extra-time to make it to the semi-finals of a European competition for the first time since 2008!

Hat-trick hero Roofe

Arfield nets v Celtic

More glory followed with another extra-time victory, this time over Celtic in the Scottish Cup semi-final! The Gers were 1-0 down but came back to send the match into extra-time before clinching their place in the final for the first time since 2016! The month ended with a 3-1 win over Motherwell, despite having Leon Balogun sent off, before losing to RB Leipzig in the Europa League semi-final first leg.

RANGERS' RESULTS

03/04	PRE	Rangers	1-2	Celtic
07/04	UEL	Braga	1-0	Rangers
10/04	PRE	St. Mirren	0-4	Rangers
14/04	UEL	Rangers	(E) 3-1	Braga
17/04	FAC	Celtic	1-2 (E)	Rangers
23/04	PRE	Motherwell	1-3	Rangers
28/04	UEL	RB Leipzig	1-0	Rangers

MAN OF THE MONTH!

KEMAR ROOFE The Gers forward had endured a tough season, but scored a hat-trick v St. Mirren before grabbing the winner against Braga. Hero!

DID YOU KNOW?

Rangers' win over Celtic in the Scottish Cup meant Giovanni van Bronckhorst hadn't lost a match in the competition as either a Gers player or manager!

SCOTTISH CUP FINAL 2022

WINNERS 2021-22

MAY
MEGA MOMENTS!

Party time after beating RB Leipzig

May is the month where trophies are won, and The Gers had the chance to make history! It started with a draw against arch-rivals Celtic that all but ended the club's hopes of retaining their league title. There were bigger prizes on offer however, and a wonderful night at Ibrox saw Rangers defeat RB Leipzig 3–1 to qualify for their first European final since 2008 – an incredible adventure!

Three league wins over Dundee United, Ross County and Hearts meant the side ended the league season with 89 points, just four behind Celtic, but two massive opportunities still lay ahead!

Penalty shootout heartbreak

First up was the Europa League final against Eintracht Frankfurt. The match was a tense one in the Seville heat and, with Aribo scoring the opening goal, it looked like The Gers had a great chance. However a Frankfurt equaliser sent the match to extra-time and then penalties. Unfortunately, Aaron Ramsey missed the only penalty in the shootout, leading to another defeat in a European final!

Just three days later, a tired Rangers team took to the field at Hampden Park against Hearts in the Scottish Cup final and despite another dose of extra-time, goals from Ryan Jack and Scott Wright saw the side lift the trophy and end the season on a high. What a campaign it was!

MAN OF THE MONTH!

CALVIN BASSEY The final gong of the season goes to the 22-year-old defender. His impressive performances all season were acknowledged with back-to-back Man of the Match performances in the Europa League and Scottish Cup finals! He definitely has a bright future ahead of him!

DID YOU KNOW?

Rangers triumphed in the Scottish Cup for the 34th time after beating Hearts, and it was their first success in the competition since 2009 – a 13-year drought!

RANGERS' RESULTS

Date	Comp	Home	Score	Away
01/05	PRE	Celtic	1-1	Rangers
05/05	UEL	Rangers	3-1	RB Leipzig
08/05	PRE	Rangers	2-0	Dundee United
11/05	PRE	Rangers	4-1	Ross County
14/05	PRE	Hearts	1-3	Rangers
18/05	UEL	Eintracht Frankfurt	[P] 1-1	Rangers
21/05	FAC	Rangers	[E] 2-0	Hearts

EUROPA LEAGUE LEGENDS

Check out some of the best stats behind Rangers' memorable run to the 2022 Europa League final!

3 — Ryan Kent and Joe Aribo set up three goals each, placing them joint-second in the tournament assist charts!

7 — Skipper James Tavernier was the competition's top scorer with seven goals!

1,320 — Three Rangers players – Tavernier, Allan McGregor and Connor Goldson – played 1,320 minutes of action, more than any other player!

40

Aged 40 years and 107 days, goalkeeper McGregor became the oldest player to play a Europa League final, and only the third player over 40 to appear in a major European final!

42

No keeper made more Europa League saves than McGregor – the 40-year-old legend kept out 42 shots in total!

3

Rangers had three players in the EL Team of the Season – Tavernier, Calvin Bassey and Ryan Kent – only winners Eintracht Frankfurt had more!

15

Tavernier also became the highest-scoring Englishman in Europa League history with 15, overtaking Harry Kane and ex-Rangers striker Jermain Defoe!

101

The right-back was a defensive beast too, with 101 ball recoveries – way more than any other player!

35

Tavernier also completed 35 crosses throughout the campaign – only Filip Kostic got more!

10 JAMES TAVERNIER FACTS!

Check out the story of Rangers' heroic right-back and skipper!

1 The wicked full-back started his career in England with Newcastle and made his professional debut when he was just 17!

2 Tavernier joined Rangers in the summer of 2015, and scored on his debut with a sick free-kick against Hibernian in the Scottish Challenge Cup!

3 He had a dream end to his first season – he netted the goal that sealed the Championship title, and scored in the Challenge Cup final!

4 He was the Europa League's top goalscorer in 2021–22 – no defender has finished top of the charts in a European comp since Barcelona's Ronald Koeman in the 1993–94 Champions League!

5 Ex-manager Steven Gerrard handed him the captain's armband ahead of the 2018–19 season, and he scored in his first game as skipper!

6 Tavernier won the Scottish PFA Players' Player of the Year after leading Rangers to their first title for ten years in 2020–21!

7 By the end of 2021–22, Tavernier had bagged 83 Rangers goals – only record appearance-maker John Greig has scored more from defence!

8 Only three players – Barry Ferguson, Steven Davis and Allan McGregor – have played more games for Rangers this century. Legend!

9 He's always had goals in him – he hit ten in his first 19 games for The Gers! Not many right-backs can claim that kind of return!

10 His younger brother Marcus is also a footballer, and joined Bournemouth from Middlesbrough last summer!

FOLLOW MATCH!

FOR LOADS OF AWESOME FOOTY NEWS, TRANSFER GOSSIP, VIDEOS & BANTER!

instagram.com/
matchmagofficial

tiktok.com/
matchmagofficial

twitter.com/
matchmagazine

facebook.com/
matchmagazine

youtube.com/matchymovie

snapchat.com/add/
matchmagazine

WICKED WEBSITE: WWW.MATCHFOOTBALL.CO.UK

RANGERS LIFT EURO SILVERWARE!

RANGERS	**3**
Stein 23, Johnston 40, 49	

DYNAMO MOSCOW	**2**
Eshtrekov 60, Makhovikov 87	

Date: May 24, 1972

Stadium: Nou Camp, Barcelona

Competition: European Cup Winners' Cup final

What happened? Rangers' greatest-ever European moment! The Gers had to overcome German giants Bayern Munich in the semi-final before taking on Dynamo Moscow in Barcelona in the final. Colin Stein and a double from Willie Johnston put them 3-0 up before a late Dynamo fightback. A nervy finish followed but the team held on to lift their first European trophy at the third time of asking, having lost two European Cup Winners' Cup finals in the 1960s!

What happened next? Rangers fans invaded the pitch in celebration, meaning that captain John Greig had to collect the trophy inside the stadium away from the pitch! The celebrations proved to be costly for The Gers, though – they were handed a one-year ban from Europe as a result so couldn't defend their trophy, and didn't reach another European final until 2008!

WORDSEARCH

Can you find the names of Rangers' top 30 goalscorers of all time?

```
Q J Y S N P T E W M M U T Q K E Q C C S B E V W E H I Z G S
M Y I R E R L K U M R A B K G T T N C U M O R T O N Y P P V
A X L K W G B J E S P A N H E X I R E I D X R Y F N D I O Z
R N I Q Z I K P A W L T Q O H M O U C B E E X I O U S F O X
S G R V D M P U Z D G D R B O T K G R U T H J T P V O Z C Q
H C P Q O H F F T B U S O P P H A M I L T O N N B R G J C A
A L E J G O A K G Q H B F D R K Y H E J J R H I A H R A M T
L D O K O X J O H N S T O N E L A A Z Y O Q X L A Z E E K F
L K F F V N J N G M F D G W B M R T J H E N L M R Z I J M I
B U U O T Q L W K H N E G B V P Q E T D S I D M C A G O Y B
F O L P P F T Z L A U X I J F T X L G Z M S W C H I Q P H R
T C C S C O O T R J F B M E S F W E U E D Q Z P I X W O K T
H B A I Q U G B E K Z Z B P G Q Z Y T H U I N H B Y U O T O
C E I M B O I U M G D H X A W H I L Y P S K T E A M X M U J
O O R P O X S L M Q I G T A R P Q L R A N S O R L W O C B Q
N B N S Y U W H G B I J V S K D B G S N U E I S D X N P H W
U M S O D G F Q F Y Q P R K D Q S H Q K U Y M O Q A Z H W H
W N P N D Q V H E N D E R S O N I C Q C L Z U N M Z W A I B
B V D X C C T W Y D F D Q H Y P K V X K H M R I C C V I E V
G B J L T I Q S J B S O P I N V D V A H S P R Z C S M L P U
U T H F M G S H S J G B R L P P I S F X Y Y A P O V B U J Q
P P I S O O B K A P K R D R I Q X E G S Z U Y F I G U T G J
X E F S L J O H N S T O N K E N K G D M H L Z J S P K U O S
E F B E Y Z C E J O S S L S O S G V M I X I O G T A A F K F
Z O R E O K R G G D G E H S E L T R H T E P N B V R F R A C
Z O F M B E U T V I Q Y L H O I Q O X H D I T T F L K V Q U
M E F L L J O B P T T I D O O F R O N G M D S F I A K Y T B
K F G L K W X L R M W Z P E N M G J N E K K R G C N K P Q C
H K I Z W R E I H O I V V F Z Z I E L L E X A X D E X V C R
N M N C U N N I N G H A M S S J P F K W Q J B A W S K X Y V
```

Archibald	Forrest	Johnston	Millar	Reid
Boyd	Greig	Johnstone	Miller	Simpson
Brand	Hamilton	Marshall	Morelos	Smith
Cairns	Hateley	McCoist	Morton	Smith
Cunningham	Henderson	McPhail	Murray	Thornton
Fleming	Hubbard	McPherson	Parlane	Wilson

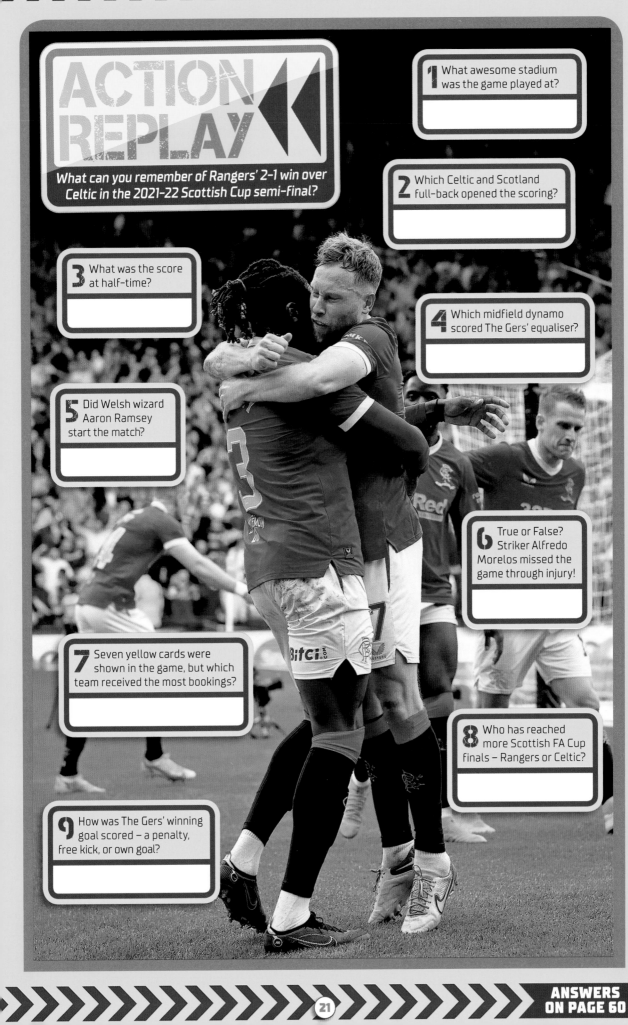

ACTION REPLAY

What can you remember of Rangers' 2–1 win over Celtic in the 2021–22 Scottish Cup semi-final?

1 What awesome stadium was the game played at?

2 Which Celtic and Scotland full-back opened the scoring?

3 What was the score at half-time?

4 Which midfield dynamo scored The Gers' equaliser?

5 Did Welsh wizard Aaron Ramsey start the match?

6 True or False? Striker Alfredo Morelos missed the game through injury!

7 Seven yellow cards were shown in the game, but which team received the most bookings?

8 Who has reached more Scottish FA Cup finals – Rangers or Celtic?

9 How was The Gers' winning goal scored – a penalty, free kick, or own goal?

ANSWERS ON PAGE 60

SCOTTISH WINNERS

Take a look at the awesome numbers behind Rangers' latest trophy win!

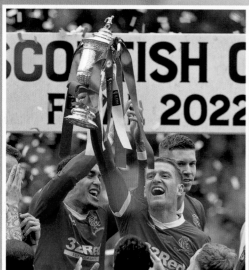

3 Fashion Sakala was Rangers' top scorer in the competition with three goals!

4 The late win over Hearts in the cup final was the fourth time in 11 games that Rangers had gone all the way to extra-time!

121 In total it was the club's 121st trophy, cementing Rangers' status as Britain's most successful club!

CUP

13
The last time Rangers had won the Scottish Cup was back in 2009 – this victory ended a 13-year wait!

34
This was the 34th time that Rangers lifted the Scottish Cup – only Celtic have won it more!

6
Giovanni van Bronckhorst lifted his first trophy since returning to Scotland, but his sixth in total – he won five as a Rangers player, including two Scottish Cups!

3
Ryan Jack and Scott Wright bagged the goals in the 2–0 win, with the strikes coming within three minutes of each other!

66
This game capped a mammoth campaign for Rangers – it was their 66th game of the season in all competitions. Wow!

JOINING THE GERS

Van Bronckhorst joined Rangers from Dutch club Feyenoord in the summer of 1998. New Dutch manager Dick Advocaat was looking to sign a lot of players from his home country, and GvB became one of the first of this new era! Costing £5.5m, he was one of the most expensive players in Scotland at the time, and is still one of Rangers' biggest signings ever. Wowzers!

DEBUT GOAL

Van Bronckhorst made his debut for The Gers in a UEFA Cup qualifying match against Irish side Shelbourne. It was supposed to be an easy game for the Scottish giants, until Shelbourne took a shock 3–0 lead! Advocaat looked like he was in trouble but epic goals from Jorg Albertz, Gabriel Amato and a debut strike from GvB gave Rangers a 5–3 victory!

FIRST TROPHY

The Dutchman's first trophy at Ibrox arrived in the November of his first season. A 2–1 victory over St. Johnstone in the 1998 League Cup final was the first piece of silverware for Advocaat, and the first major trophy that Rangers had won since the league title in May 1997!

TREBLE SUCCESS

GvB played in the 1999 Scottish Cup final as The Gers won 1–0 against arch-rivals Celtic to secure a remarkable treble in Advocaat's first season in charge! It was the first time Rangers had won all three trophies in the same campaign since 1993 and Van Bronckhorst made a staggering 53 appearances, scoring ten goals. What a debut season in Scotland!

Scrapbook!

DOMINATING SCOTLAND

Rangers won the title again in 1999-00, and in that season's Scottish Cup final The Gers thumped Aberdeen 4-0 at Hampden, with Van Bronckhorst scoring the first goal to set up an amazing win! Before the match, the Rangers fans all wore orange as support for Advocaat and the Dutch players at the club, and it made for an incredible atmosphere!

MOVING ON

Van Bronckhorst's final season at Ibrox wasn't as successful as the first two as the club finished trophyless for the first time since 1997-98. He did score three goals in the 2000-01 Champions League though, which caught the attention of Arsenal, who snapped up the Dutchman for £8.5m in June 2001!

RETURN AS MANAGER

Van Bronckhort returned to Ibrox in November 2022, 21 years after he first left The Gers, to take over from the Aston Villa-bound Steven Gerrard. He was a popular appointment with the Rangers faithful, with many hoping he could win as many trophies as he did when he played for the club!

DREAM DEBUT

The Dutchman's first match in charge came in the Europa League group stage against Sparta Prague. The Gers won 2-0, with both goals scored by a rejuvenated Alfredo Morelos as Van Bronckhorst got off to the perfect start. The result meant his side qualified for the knockout stage of the competition!

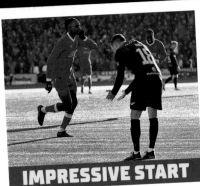

IMPRESSIVE START

Van Bronckhorst won his opening seven league games in charge of The Gers, and the supporters were loving it! Midfield dynamo Joe Aribo grabbed three goals during the epic run and the club looked on course to win another league title!

PROGRESS IN EUROPE

Rangers had been phenomenal in Europe under Steven Gerrard, but GvB took it up another notch by guiding The Gers to absolutely massive wins. In the first match after Christmas, they were huge underdogs against German giants Borussia Dortmund, but smashed them 6-4 on aggregate!

EURO HEARTBREAK

More European victories against Red Star Belgrade, Braga and RB Leipzig meant that GvB led The Gers all the way to the Europa League final – the club's first Euro final since 2008! Hopes were high, but the night ended in a heartbreaking penalty shootout defeat to Eintracht Frankfurt, leaving the fans and players devastated!

SCOTTISH CUP SUCCESS

Rangers hadn't won the Scottish Cup in 13 years until Gio arrived, and a famous 2-0 victory in extra-time over Hearts made sure The Gers had a trophy to celebrate! Despite having already played 120 minutes in the Europa League final just three days earlier, Rangers kept on going to secure the win. GvB has never lost a Scottish Cup match as player or manager for the club. Wow!

RANGERS' REVENGE!

RANGERS — 2
Vidmar 34, Reyna 75

PARMA — 0

Date: August 11, 1999

Stadium: Ibrox Stadium, Glasgow

Competition: Champions League qualifier

What happened? One of the biggest results in Rangers' European history! A year earlier, a star-studded Parma side had defeated The Gers on their way to winning the UEFA Cup, but manager Dick Advocaat made sure it didn't happen again! Epic goals from Australian Tony Vidmar and American Claudio Reyna gave them a 2-0 victory as Ibrox exploded with noise!

What happened next? Rangers sealed a 2-1 aggregate win to reach the Champions League group stage after a three-year absence! Sadly though, conceding a 90th-minute equaliser at home to Bundesliga giants Bayern Munich cost them qualification from the group!

RANGERS

DREAM TEAM

Select your favourite line-up from Rangers' greatest-ever players for the chance to win an awesome prize! Go...

DREAM TEAM
GOALKEEPERS!

STEFAN KLOS
1998-2007

Klos was one of the finest keepers in Europe when he signed for Rangers in 1998, winning the Champions League with Borussia Dortmund a year earlier. The German left The Gers after winning ten major honours and making 298 appearances. His nickname was 'Der Goalie', a reference to the man he replaced, Andy Goram!

CHRIS WOODS
1986-1991

Woods was signed by Graeme Souness in 1986 and made the No.1 shirt his own for the next five seasons! The Englishman didn't concede a goal for nearly 1,200 minutes between November 1986 and January 1987, a British record at the time. Wow!

ALLAN McGREGOR
1998-2012, 2018-PRESENT

McGregor made his debut as a fresh-faced youngster against Forfar in 2002 and at 40, was still The Gers No.1! His penalty save against Celtic in 2011 went down as one of the moments of the season as he won his fourth league title. A true Ibrox legend!

ANDY GORAM
1991-1998

Nicknamed 'The Goalie', Goram was a regular feature in the side that won nine titles in a row, and many think he's the finest goalkeeper to have played for The Gers! He was inducted into the Scottish Football Hall of Fame in 2010!

PETER McCLOY
1970-1986

McCloy was the Rangers keeper when the European Cup Winners' Cup was won in 1972 and he won everything during his amazing 16-year spell at the club. With 535 games, he's ninth on Rangers' all-time record appearance list!

BEST OF THE REST...   CHECK OUT THESE OTHER SUPERSTARS!

RONALD WATERREUS
2005-2006

BILLY RITCHIE
1955-1967

BOBBY BROWN
1946-1956

ALLY MAXWELL
1992-1995

NEIL ALEXANDER
2008-2013

DREAM TEAM
FULL-BACKS!

JAMES TAVERNIER
2015-PRESENT

The penalty king! Tavernier led Rangers to title number 55 and then the 2022 Scottish Cup, ending major droughts in both. He also won the Europa League Golden Boot during the club's run to last season's final – not bad for a right-back! Tav has more years ahead of him, but he's already a Gers legend and one of the best captains Rangers have ever had!

ARTHUR NUMAN
1998-2003

Numan was one of the many Dutch players to sign for The Gers under manager Dick Advocaat and was very popular during his spell at the club, winning two domestic trebles in just five years! At £4.5m, Numan remains one of the clubs most expensive players ever!

JOHN GREIG
1961-1978

Quite simply, Mr. Rangers. Greig played every position possible for the club, but he was best known for his spell at left-back. He was voted 'The Greatest-Ever Ranger' in 1999, won three domestic trebles during his playing career, and holds the record for most appearances for The Gers with 755. Legend!

SANDY JARDINE
1966-1982

One of the finest right-backs in the club's history. Jardine won 14 trophies at The Gers, including the European Cup Winners' Cup in 1972 before finishing his career at Hearts. Jardine holds the record for most World Cup appearances by a Gers player with four, at the 1974 and 1978 tournaments with Scotland!

FERNANDO RICKSEN
2000-2006

An unknown when he arrived, Ricksen left Rangers having won every domestic trophy! He was class in midfield but even better at right-back! He was captain for 'Helicopter Sunday', which saw The Gers snatch the league from Celtic on the last day of the season!

BEST OF THE REST...   CHECK OUT THESE OTHER SUPERSTARS!

DAVID ROBERTSON
1991-1997

SASA PAPAC
2006-2012

LEE WALLACE
2011-2019

GARY STEVENS
1988-1994

BORNA BARISIC
2018-PRESENT

DREAM TEAM
CENTRE-BACKS!

LORENZO AMORUSO
1997-2003

The long-haired Italian was a rock-solid defender, but also had such a wicked shot that he used to score tons of free-kicks during his Rangers career! He was also a goal threat with his head, and nodded home the winner in the Scottish Cup Final in his last ever Gers match – what a way to bow out!

GEORGE YOUNG
1941-1957

Young was nicknamed 'Corky' because he used to carry a lucky champagne cork around with him! It seemed to help as he won 12 trophies with The Gers and was the first Scottish player to win over 50 caps, a true Rangers icon!

DAVID WEIR
2007-2012

Weir's initial six-month loan move turned into a five-year trophy-laden spell, and he captained the side to three league titles in a row! He retired at the grand old age of 42, with team-mates half his age playing alongside him!

TERRY BUTCHER
1986-1990

English legend Butcher turned Rangers' fortunes around, helping the team win their first league title in nine long years in 1987! He was one of the best defenders in the world at the time and he played in two World Cups for England!

RICHARD GOUGH
1987-1997, 1997-1998

Gough led Rangers to nine league titles in a row between 1988 and 1997 – an amazing achievement! He was a brilliant defender with strong tackling and commitment, and was a proper fans' favourite! He left to move to America, but returned when the club needed him, displaying his loyalty to The Gers!

BEST OF THE REST... CHECK OUT THESE OTHER SUPERSTARS!

CRAIG MOORE
1994-1998, 1999-2005

MADJID BOUGHERRA
2008-2011

CARLOS CUELLAR
2007-2008

JOHN BROWN
1988-1997

CONNOR GOLDSON
2018-present

DREAM TEAM
MIDFIELDERS!

PAUL GASCOIGNE

1995-1998

Gazza was one of the best players in the world when Rangers signed him from Lazio for £4.3m in 1995. He played his part in two title wins and scored some epic goals against rivals Celtic, but his cheeky humour often got him into bother – he was once booked after the ref dropped his yellow card and Gazza picked it up and pretended to book him!

BARRY FERGUSON

1997-2003, 2005-2009

The Scottish legend will go down as one of the finest captains The Gers have ever had, winning a remarkable 15 major trophies at Ibrox! His canny ability to score goals from midfield made him a big fans' favourite and, even though he left for a spell at Blackburn Rovers in 2003, he was welcomed back with open arms in 2005 for a second spell!

RONALD DE BOER

2000-2004

It's not often Rangers sign a player from Barcelona, especially when they're one of the best in the world! De Boer was a magician who could give defenders nightmares with his flair, dribbling and creativity, while his goalscoring ability was amazing too, with 40 goals in just four years – including some absolute bangers!

IAN FERGUSON

1988-2000

The Glaswegian was a brilliant midfielder, and one of only three players to be involved in all of Rangers' nine consecutive titles of the '90s! His fighting spirit and never-say-die attitude carried The Gers to loads of trophies during his 12-year spell, and he left Ibrox in 2000 with a total of 18 winners' medals – incredible!

STEVEN DAVIS

2008-2012, 2019-PRESENT

Davis is one of the few men to appear in two European finals for The Gers and his professionalism throughout his two spells at the club is second to none. Even at 37 he can still cover every blade of grass – it feels like he could carry on playing football forever!

BEST OF THE REST...
CHECK OUT THESE OTHER SUPERSTARS!

IAN DURRANT
1985-1998

STUART McCALL
1991-1998

GIOVANNI V. BRONCKHORST
1998-2001

RAY WILKINS
1987-1989

GRAEME SOUNESS
1986-1991

DREAM TEAM
WINGERS!

BRIAN LAUDRUP

1994-1998

You have to be a special player to have a match named after you, and that's what happened to Laudrup during his four years at Rangers! The great Dane scored twice and set up another three in Rangers' 5-1 win over Hearts in the 1996 Scottish Cup final, which is why it's now known as the 'Laudrup Final'!

JIM BAXTER

1960-1965, 1969-1970

'Slim Jim', as Baxter was dubbed, was famed for his ability to beat defenders over and over again. He's not just a legend to Rangers fans either – Scotland supporters loved the unpredictable winger after he tormented the English defence on the way to a 3-2 victory against the then world champions in 1967!

WILLIE HENDERSON

1960-1972

Henderson was one of Rangers' first great wingers, and should have been in the team that lifted the European Cup Winners' Cup in 1972, but he left Ibrox just before the Barcelona final. At his peak, the wing wizard was regarded as one of the best dribblers in Britain for his ability to tie defenders in knots!

JORG ALBERTZ

1996-2001

There's a reason Albertz was dubbed 'The Hammer' – opposition keepers were terrified of getting in the way of one his unstoppable shots! The German's lethal left foot meant that he was a threat from anywhere on the pitch – as rivals Celtic found out when he crashed in a long-range free-kick against them to help seal the 1998-99 league title!

DAVIE COOPER

1977-1989

Cooper's left foot was like a wand – wherever he wanted the ball to go, that's where it went! He was famous for his rock-hard shot and dead-ball skills during his time at The Gers, and defenders must have hated the sight of him running at them with the ball at his feet. One of the club's finest ever players!

BEST OF THE REST...   CHECK OUT THESE OTHER SUPERSTARS!

MARK WALTERS
1987-1991

NEIL McCANN
1998-2003

PETER LOVENKRANDS
2000-2006

DAVIE WILSON
1956-1967

ANDREI KANCHELSKIS
1998-2002

DREAM TEAM
STRIKERS!

KRIS BOYD

2006-2010, 2014-2015

The perfect poacher! Whenever Rangers needed a goal, Boyd was the man to rely on and he banged in a whopping 138 goals in only 234 games! With his skills and eye for goal, it's no wonder he netted so many times and helped The Gers to a bucket load of trophies!

DEREK JOHNSTONE

1970-1983, 1985-1986

Johnstone, or DJ as he was better known, made a name for himself by scoring the winner against Celtic in the League Cup final in 1970 when he should have still been at school, aged 16! His skills allowed him to play either as a striker or a defender, and he's in Rangers' all-time top ten for both goals and appearances!

ALLY McCOIST

1983-1998

Super Ally scored an amazing 355 goals for Rangers in 15 years, more than any other player in the club's history! To give you an idea of how prolific McCoist was at his best, he's one of only five players to win the European Golden Shoe in back-to-back years, alongside Lionel Messi, Cristiano Ronaldo, Thierry Henry and Robert Lewandowski!

MARK HATELEY

1990-1995, 1997

Hateley formed a dream duo with McCoist during his time at Ibrox! The long-haired Englishman was unstoppable in the air and was capable of scoring all types of goals, from close-range tap-ins to 30-yard volleys! He won the PFA and FWA Player of the Year awards in 1993-94 after scoring 30 goals!

COLIN STEIN

1968-1972, 1975-1978

Stein has legendary status at Ibrox for being one of the goalscorers in Rangers' only victory in a European final, netting the opener in the 1972 Cup Winners' Cup win! He's also in Scotland's record books as the last person to score four goals in a game for the country back in 1970!

BEST OF THE REST... CHECK OUT THESE OTHER SUPERSTARS!

NIKICA JELAVIC
2010-2012

MICHAEL MOLS
1999-2004

DADO PRSO
2004-2007

NACHO NOVO
2004-2010

GORDON DURIE
1993-2000

DREAM TEAM
MY ALL-TIME RANGERS XI!

You've seen our shortlist of Rangers legends – now pick your dream line-up!

GOALKEEPER
Andy Goram

RIGHT-BACK
Sandy Jardine

CENTRE-BACK
Gough

CENTRE-BACK
Terry Butcher

LEFT-BACK
John Greig

WINGER
Davie Cooper

MIDFIELDER
Gascoigne

MIDFIELDER
Ian Ferguson

WINGER
Jim Baxter

STRIKER
Mols

STRIKER
McCoist

WIN! A PRO COMPACT XBOX CONTROLLER!

Use the pitch graphic above to pick your favourite Rangers XI, fill out your details, then email a photo of this page to:
match.magazine@kelsey.co.uk
with the subject line Rangers Dream Team, and one lucky winner will bag this cool prize!
Closing date: Janaury 21, 2023.

For loads more information and cool gaming accessories, head over to *nacongaming.com* and follow *@Nacon*

nacon

Name: Sam Coghill

Age: 11

Address: 13 Juniper Drive, Thurso, Scotland

Postcode: KW14 7AS

Email: Sam.coghill@icloud.com

TERRY BUTCHER

Italia '90 was the best World Cup for Rangers players with seven of their heroes on show! None of them shone more than Butcher though, who was the rock at the heart of the England defence that reached the semi-finals!

ERIC CALDOW

The ex-Scotland defender made history as the first-ever Rangers player to feature at a World Cup! In 1958 Caldow travelled to Sweden and started all three matches as they exited in the group stage!

BRIAN LAUDRUP

Laudrup was one of the most gifted players to ever play for Rangers, and he proved it at the 1998 World Cup in France! He scored two goals and set up three more as Denmark reached the quarter-finals, and was named in the All-star Team – the only active Gers player to ever do so. Legend!

RANGERS' WORLD CUP STORIES

The 2022 World Cup in Qatar got us reminiscing about the Rangers superstars to have been involved at previous tournaments...

GIOVANNI VAN BRONCKHORST

The Gers manager can claim to have scored one of the all-time great World Cup goals! GVB played every game as Netherlands' reached the 2010 final in South Africa, and banged in an absolute thunderbolt against Uruguay in the semis – if you've never seen it, check it out on YouTube!

CLAUDIO CANIGGIA

Rangers fans loved Caniggia during his time at the club, but his trip to Japan and South Korea in 2002 was a disaster! Not only did he not play a minute of Argentina's campaign, he was sent off while still on the bench for dissent towards the ref!

MAGIC EUROPEAN MOMENTS NO. 3

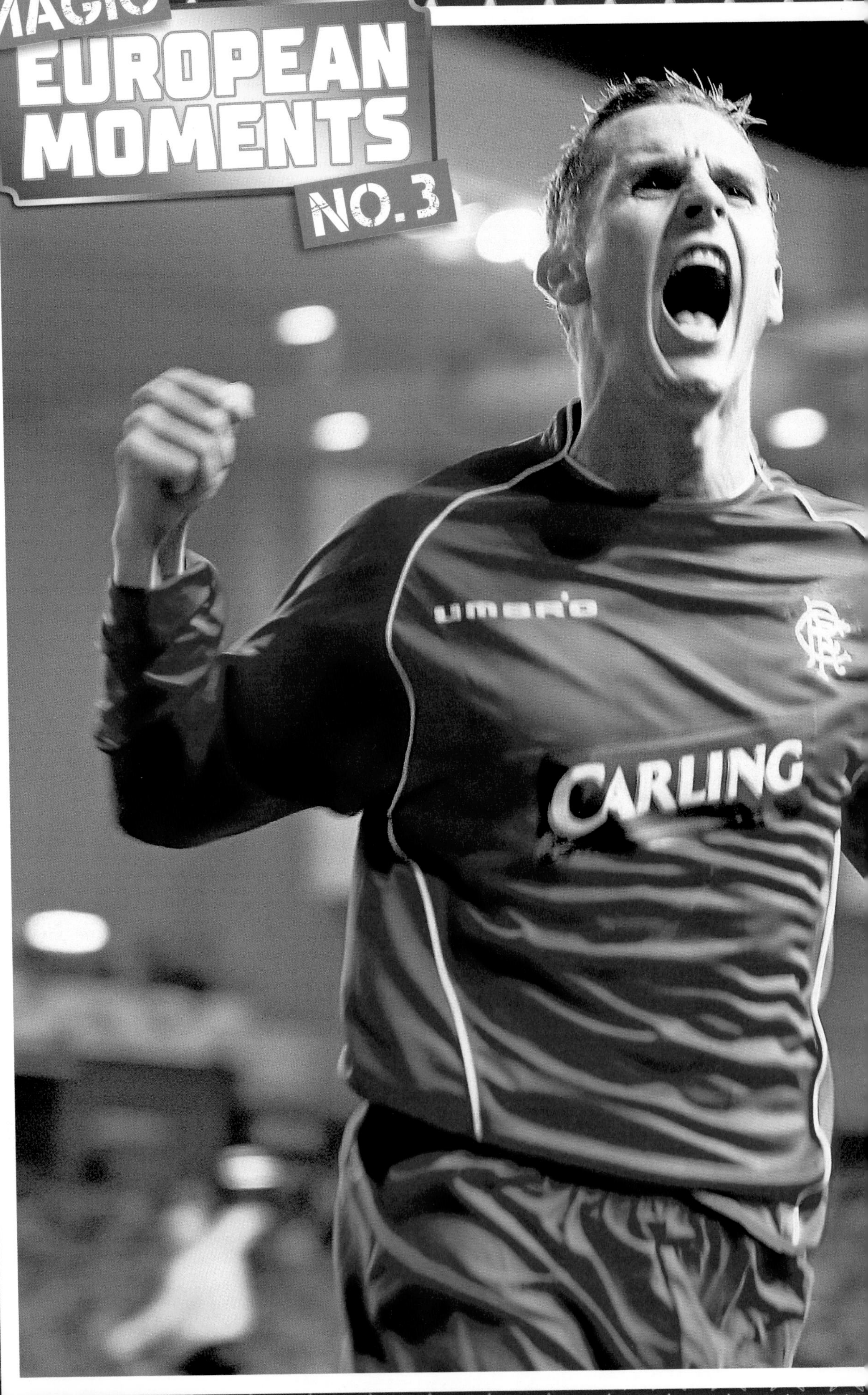

HISTORY MAKERS!

RANGERS — 1
Lovenkrands 38

INTER MILAN — 1
Adriano 30

Date: December 6, 2005

Stadium: Ibrox Stadium, Glasgow

Competition: Champions League group stage

What happened? Rangers went into their clash with Italian giants Inter Milan knowing that a draw would make them the first Scottish side to reach the Champions League knockout stages. Brazilian striker Adriano nearly ruined the party, but Peter Lovenkrands scored the equaliser as a famous night in Glasgow ended with 1-1 draw, ensuring The Gers made history!

What happened next? Rangers' Euro journey ended in the last 16 as Spanish club Villarreal knocked them out on their way to the semi-finals. This was the first and, so far, only time Rangers have made it to the Champions League knockouts – hopefully that changes soon!

John Lundstram

Connor Goldson

Glen Kamara

James Tavernier

ODD ONE OUT!

Which of these awesome Rangers stars was not signed from an English club?

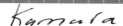

Kamara

Ryan Kent

Scott Arfield

5 QUESTIONS ON...

STEVEN DAVIS

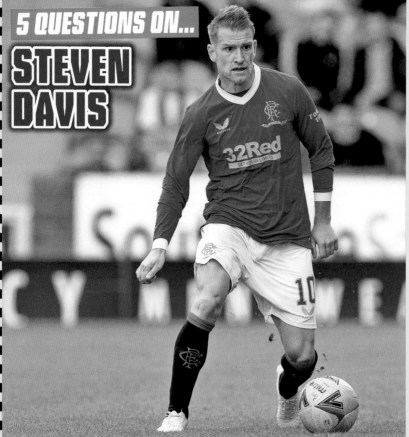

1 How much did Rangers pay for Davis when they signed him from Fulham in 2008 - £500,000, £1m, £3m or £5m?

3m

2 Davis was one of two Rangers players to start in both the 2008 UEFA Cup final and the 2022 Europa League final - who was the other?

A. Mcregor

3 The classy Northern Ireland midfield master has played for three English clubs - Aston Villa, Fulham and who else?

Southhampton

4 How many goals did Davis score in Rangers' awesome Premiership-winning campaign in 2020-21 - none, five or ten?

None

5 True or False? Davis is the most capped Northern Ireland player of all time!

True

NAME THE TEAM

Can you remember Rangers' starting XI from their awesome 2021-22 Scottish FA Cup final victory over Hearts?

1. Striker

Aribo

2. Centre-back

Balogun

3. Centre-back

Goldson

4. Left-back

Bassey

5. Goalkeeper

mcLaughlin

6. Winger

Diallo

7. Midfielder

Lundstrum

8. Midfielder

Davis

9. Right-back

Tavanier

10. Midfielder

Arfield

11. Winger

Kent

ANSWERS ON PAGE 60

BEHIND THE SCENES AT...
IBROX

IBROX GATES

BROOMLOAN STAND TIFO

THE WORLD'S MOST SUCCESSFUL FOOTBALL CLUB

1972
EUROPEAN CUP WINNERS' CUP

55
LEAGUE TITLES

33
SCOTTISH CUP WINS

27
LEAGUE CUP WINS

THE HONOURS BOARD

We take a closer look at Rangers' famous old stadium!

THE ENTRANCE

THE DRESSING ROOM

EUROPEAN MOMENTS

NO. 4

LYON · 0

RANGERS · 3

McCulloch 23, Cousin 48, Beasley 53

Date: October 2, 2007

Stadium: Stade de Gerland, Lyon

Competition: Champions League group stage

What happened? Lyon had won the French title a staggering six times in a row and would make it seven by the end of the 2007-08 season, so they were heavy favourites! That didn't trouble Rangers though, as goals from Lee McCulloch, Daniel Cousin and DaMarcus Beasley gave them an easy 3-0 win and one of the club's greatest European nights! This was only Rangers' third victory away from home against a French side in Europe – and what a win it was!

What happened next? Despite the famous victory, the Gers finished third after defeats against Barcelona, Stuttgart and Lyon and dropped into the UEFA Cup – where a new fairy-tale adventure was about to begin...

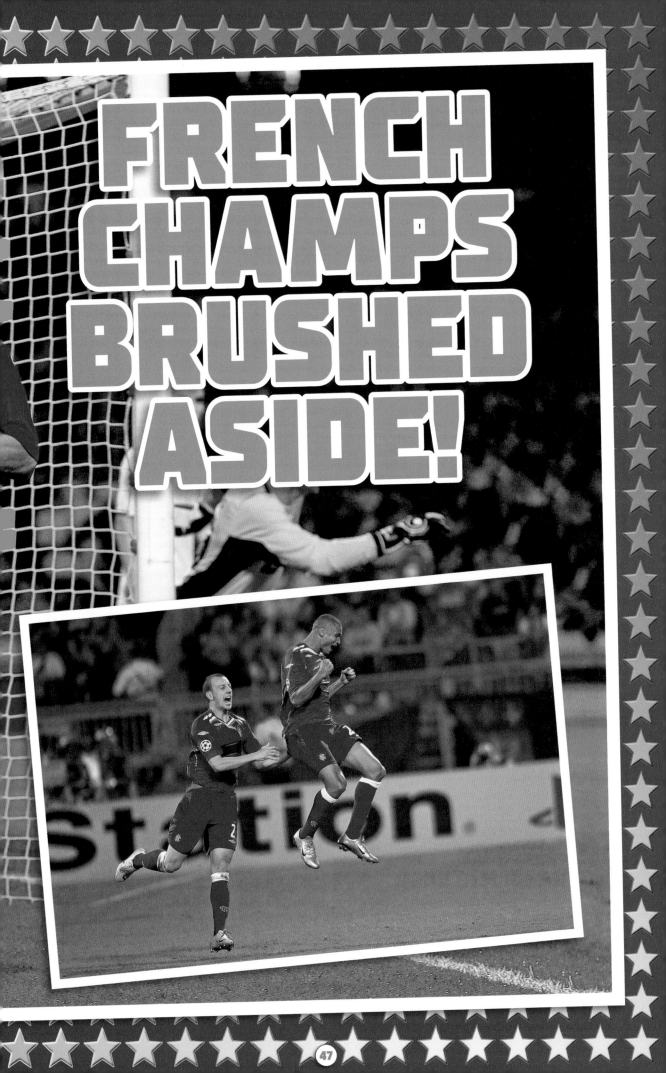

FRENCH CHAMPS BRUSHED ASIDE!

RANGERS' NEW SIGNINGS!

Take a look at some of the new players to arrive at Ibrox in the summer of 2022!

MALIK TILLMAN

Forward ★ Bayern Munich

German giants Bayern have one of the best academies in the world, so Rangers have high hopes for their new loan signing! He made his debut for USA in 2022 and will be aiming to play at the Qatar World Cup!

RABBI MATONDO

Winger ★ Schalke

Joe Aribo moving to Southampton meant that The Gers needed another rapid forward, and Matondo could be perfect! He tore up the Belgian league on loan at Cercle Brugge in 2021-22, with nine goals and two assists, and is only going to get better. He was compared to Jadon Sancho and Gareth Bale after leaving Man. City back in 2019!

RIDVAN YILMAZ

Left-back ★ Besiktas

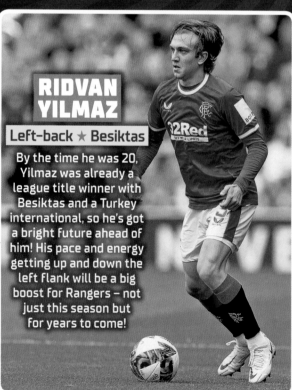

By the time he was 20, Yilmaz was already a league title winner with Besiktas and a Turkey international, so he's got a bright future ahead of him! His pace and energy getting up and down the left flank will be a big boost for Rangers – not just this season but for years to come!

ANTONIO COLAK

Striker ★ PAOK

The Croatian has played and scored all over Europe, from Germany to Poland, Sweden and Greece! Rangers are the 11th club of his career and, after bagging over 130 career goals, he could have a big impact in Scotland!

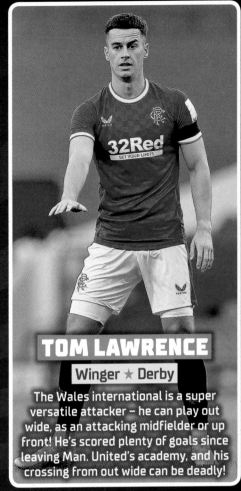

TOM LAWRENCE

Winger ★ Derby

The Wales international is a super versatile attacker – he can play out wide, as an attacking midfielder or up front! He's scored plenty of goals since leaving Man. United's academy, and his crossing from out wide can be deadly!

JOHN SOUTTAR

Centre-back ★ Hearts

Souttar has been around the Scottish Prem for ages, making his debut for Dundee United when he was only 16 to become their youngest-ever player! He's a beast in the air, but is also good with the ball at his feet!

BEN DAVIES

Centre-back ★ Liverpool

Davies was signed to replace Calvin Bassey after the Nigerian's £20 million move to Ajax, so he's got big boots to fill! Although he never made a first-team appearance for Liverpool, he was excellent in the Championship for Preston and Sheffield United, combining tough defending with a classy left foot!

We reveal the five youngsters that could be the Rangers stars of tomorrow!

RANGERS' NEXT

ALEX LOWRY
MIDFIELDER

The midfielder made his debut for The Gers at the tender age of 18 in a Scottish Cup match against Stirling Albion, and showed his class by scoring his first-ever goal in the same game! Lowry drove through the middle of the park, played a neat one-two, then slotted the ball into the bottom corner – showing just why he could be the future of Rangers' midfield!

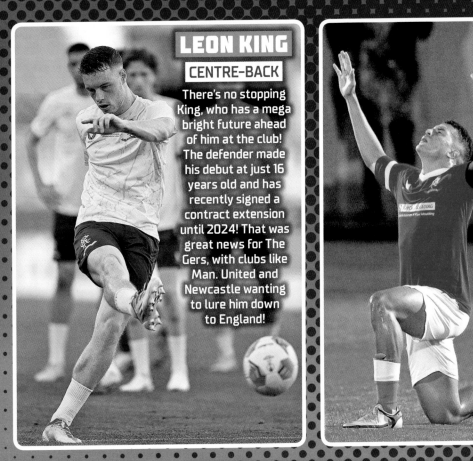

LEON KING
CENTRE-BACK

There's no stopping King, who has a mega bright future ahead of him at the club! The defender made his debut at just 16 years old and has recently signed a contract extension until 2024! That was great news for The Gers, with clubs like Man. United and Newcastle wanting to lure him down to England!

JUAN ALEGRIA
STRIKER

Alfredo Morelos won't be playing at Ibrox forever, but The Gers already have the ideal replacement in 20-year-old Alegria. The striker is like a clone of his fellow Colombian team-mate, as he showed by scoring a hat-trick for Rangers' B-team in October 2021 before joining Championship side Partick Thistle on loan. He's yet to play for the senior team, but that could change during the 2022-23 season!

GENERATION!

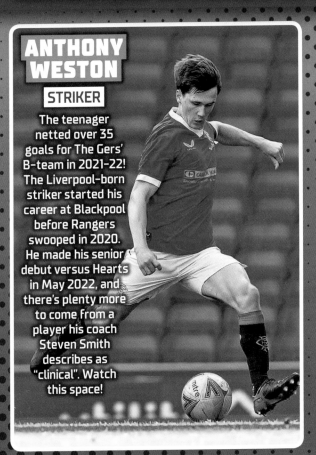

ANTHONY WESTON
STRIKER

The teenager netted over 35 goals for The Gers' B-team in 2021-22! The Liverpool-born striker started his career at Blackpool before Rangers swooped in 2020. He made his senior debut versus Hearts in May 2022, and there's plenty more to come from a player his coach Steven Smith describes as "clinical". Watch this space!

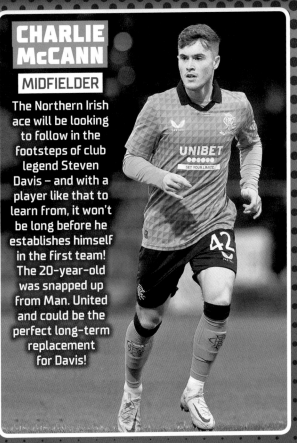

CHARLIE McCANN
MIDFIELDER

The Northern Irish ace will be looking to follow in the footsteps of club legend Steven Davis – and with a player like that to learn from, it won't be long before he establishes himself in the first team! The 20-year-old was snapped up from Man. United and could be the perfect long-term replacement for Davis!

RANGERS WOMEN

Rangers WFC had an unreal campaign in 2021-22! Check out some of the stats behind their title-winning season...

1 The 2021-22 Scottish Women's Premier League title was Rangers WFC's first-ever major honour, 14 years after the club was formed!

14 By lifting the league title, Rangers Women ended the dominance of Glasgow City, who'd won the league an incredible 14 years in a row!

0 Just like the men's side in 2020-21, Rangers WFC went the whole league campaign without losing a single game!

17 Rangers Women kept a total of 17 clean sheets during the campaign, the same number as runners-up Glasgow City!

97

They fell just short of scoring a century of goals, but banged in a whopping 97 in total – that's more than three per game on average!

86+

They only let in 11 goals, meaning they finished with the league's best goal difference too!

20

Lizzie Arnot was the club's top scorer with 20 goals – six more than team-mates Jane Ross and Kayla McCoy!

3

Rangers Women defeated arch-rivals Celtic in all three of their league games on their way to the trophy, conceding just once and scoring seven times!

93%

In addition to going unbeaten, they only dropped points in two matches, winning 25 of their 27 games. That's a win rate of 93%!

WORLDIE WOMEN

Meet the stars behind Rangers Women's record-breaking title victory!

JANE ROSS

Ross' experience played a huge role in Rangers' title win! A Scotland legend with more than 60 goals and well over 100 caps, the striker won six league titles and three Scottish Cups with Glasgow City at the start of her career, before going on to play for Swedish side Vittsjo, and in the WSL for Man. City, West Ham and Man. United!

DID YOU KNOW?
Ross was named in the 2016-17 PFA Team of the Year after helping Man. City win the WSL and League Cup in 2016, and the FA Cup in 2016-17!

LIZZIE ARNOT

Forward Arnot joined Man. United for their first-ever season in 2018-19, and helped The Red Devils reach the English WSL at the first time of asking. She returned to Scotland in 2020, and quickly found more success with Rangers by finishing as the top scorer in the club's first league title win!

DID YOU KNOW?
Arnot is in the Man. United Women's history books after scoring the club's First-ever goal, netting the winner in a 1-0 League Cup win over Liverpool!

NICOLA DOCHERTY

Docherty won every major honour in Scotland with Glasgow City, but got even better after moving down the road in February 2020! The 30-year-old defender is the rock at the heart of Rangers' defence, and her trophy-winning experience played a big part in last season's title victory!

DID YOU KNOW?
Docherty played in Scotland's first-ever game at the Women's World Cup, having helped the team qualify for the 2019 tournament in France!

RANGERS BRAIN BUSTER!

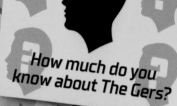

How much do you know about The Gers?

1. How many European finals have Rangers reached?

2. True or False? Giovanni van Bronckhorst is the first Dutchman to manage Rangers!

3. What African country does forward Fashion Sakala play for?

4. In what year did The Gers clinch their ninth title in a row – 1995, 1996 or 1997?

5. In what year did captain marvel James Tavernier join The Gers?

6. How many Scottish League Cups have Rangers won?

7. Which English club did Rangers sell right-back Nathan Patterson to in 2022?

8. True or False? Club legend Ally McCoist scored over 300 goals for The Gers!

9. How old is awesome goalkeeper Allan McGregor?

10. Which Dutch club did gaffer Giovanni van Bronckhorst start his managerial career with?

1 Five
2 False
3 Zambia
4 1997
5 2015
6 27
7 Everton
8 True
9 40
10 Feyrnood

WORDFIT

Fit Rangers' squad from last season's Europa League final into the grid!

Arfield	Davis	Kamara	McCann	Roofe
Aribo	Devine	Kent	McCrorie	Sands
Balogun	Diallo	King	McGregor	Tavernier
Barisic	Goldson	Lowry	McLaughlin	Wright
Bassey	Jack	Lundstram	Ramsey	

ANSWERS ON PAGE 60

FIORENTINA	**0**
RANGERS	**0**

0-0 ON AGGREGATE, RANGERS WIN 4-2 ON PENALTIES

Date: May 1, 2008

Stadium: Stadio Artemio Franchi, Florence

Competition: UEFA Cup semi-final 2nd leg

What happened? Walter Smith led the club on a fantastic run to the UEFA Cup semi-finals after Champions League disappointment. Two boring goalless draws with Fiorentina led to a nerve-racking penalty shootout – and the nerves were seriously jangling when captain Barry Ferguson missed from the spot! But, after Fiorentina missed two kicks of their own, Spanish striker Nacho Novo made himself the hero by scoring the winning penalty to end The Gers' 36-year wait for a European final!

What happened next? Unfortunately it wasn't to be for Rangers in the final at the City of Manchester Stadium. Their 64th match of the season proved to be one step too star, as Andriy Arshavin inspired Zenit to a 2-0 victory!

BACK IN THE BIG TIME!

Wordsearch — P20

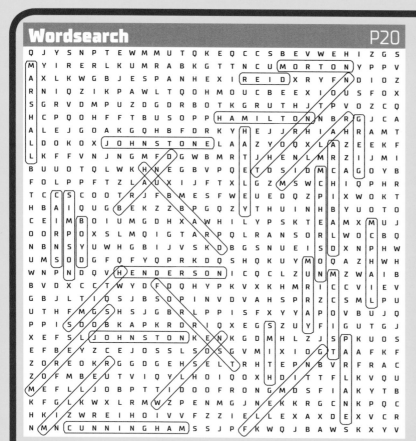

Q	J	Y	S	N	P	T	E	W	M	M	U	T	Q	K	E	Q	C	C	S	B	E	V	W	E	H	I	Z	G	S
M	Y	I	R	E	R	L	K	U	M	R	A	B	K	G	T	T	N	C	U	M	O	R	T	O	N	Y	P	P	V
A	X	L	K	W	G	B	J	E	S	P	A	N	H	E	X	I	R	E	I	D	X	R	Y	F	N	D	I	O	Z
R	N	I	Q	Z	I	K	P	A	W	L	T	Q	O	H	M	O	U	C	B	E	E	X	I	O	U	S	F	O	X
S	G	R	V	D	M	P	U	Z	D	G	D	R	B	O	T	K	G	R	U	T	H	J	T	P	V	O	Z	C	Q
H	C	P	Q	O	H	F	F	T	B	U	S	O	P	P	H	A	M	I	L	T	O	N	N	B	R	G	J	A	B
A	L	E	J	G	O	A	K	G	Q	H	B	F	D	R	K	Y	H	E	J	J	R	H	I	A	R	A	M	T
L	D	O	K	O	X	J	O	H	N	S	T	O	N	E	L	A	A	Z	Y	Q	Q	X	L	A	Z	E	E	K	F
L	K	F	F	V	N	J	N	G	M	F	D	G	W	B	M	R	T	J	H	E	N	L	M	R	Z	I	J	M	I
B	U	U	O	T	Q	L	W	K	H	N	E	G	B	V	P	Q	E	T	D	S	I	D	M	C	A	G	O	Y	B
F	O	L	P	P	F	T	Z	L	A	U	X	I	J	F	T	X	L	G	Z	M	S	W	C	H	I	Q	P	H	R
T	C	C	S	C	O	O	T	R	J	F	B	M	E	S	F	W	E	U	E	D	Q	Z	P	I	X	W	O	K	T
H	B	A	I	Q	U	G	B	E	K	Z	Z	B	P	G	Q	Z	Y	T	H	U	I	N	H	B	Y	U	O	T	O
C	E	I	M	B	O	I	U	M	G	D	X	A	W	H	I	L	Y	P	S	K	T	E	A	M	X	M	U	J	J
O	O	R	P	O	X	S	L	M	Q	I	G	T	A	R	P	Q	L	R	A	N	S	O	R	L	W	O	C	B	Q
N	B	N	S	Y	U	W	H	G	B	I	J	V	S	K	D	B	G	S	N	U	E	I	S	D	X	N	P	H	W
U	M	S	O	D	G	F	Q	F	Y	Q	P	R	K	D	Q	S	H	Q	K	Q	A	Z	H	W	H
W	N	N	D	Q	V	H	E	N	D	E	R	S	O	N	I	C	C	L	Z	U	N	M	Z	W	A	I
B	V	O	X	C	C	T	W	Y	D	F	Q	H	Y	P	K	V	K	H	M	R	I	C	C	V	I	E	V
G	B	J	L	T	I	Q	S	H	J	G	B	R	L	P	P	I	S	F	X	Y	Y	A	P	O	H	A	J
U	T	H	F	M	G	S	H	S	J	G	B	R	L	P	P	I	S	F	X	Y	Y	A	P	O	H	A	J
P	P	I	S	O	O	B	K	A	P	K	R	D	R	I	Q	X	E	G	S	Z	U	Y	F	I	G	U	T	G	J
X	E	F	S	L	J	O	H	N	S	T	O	N	K	E	N	K	G	D	M	H	L	Z	J	S	P	K	U	O	S
E	F	B	E	Y	Z	C	E	J	O	S	S	L	S	O	S	G	V	M	I	X	I	O	G	T	A	A	F	K	F
Z	O	R	E	O	K	R	G	G	D	G	E	H	S	E	L	T	R	H	T	E	P	N	B	V	R	F	R	A	C
Z	O	F	M	B	E	U	T	V	I	Q	Y	L	H	O	I	Q	O	X	H	D	I	T	T	F	L	K	V	Q	U
M	E	F	L	L	J	O	B	P	T	T	I	D	O	O	F	R	O	N	G	M	D	S	F	I	A	K	Y	T	B
K	F	G	L	K	W	X	L	R	M	W	Z	P	E	N	M	G	J	N	E	K	K	R	G	C	N	K	P	Q	C
H	K	I	Z	W	R	E	I	H	O	I	V	V	F	Z	Z	I	E	L	L	E	X	A	X	D	E	X	V	C	R
N	M	N	C	U	N	N	I	N	G	H	A	M	S	S	J	P	F	K	W	Q	J	B	A	W	S	K	X	Y	V

Action Replay — P21

1. Hampden Park
2. Greg Taylor
3. 0-0
4. Scott Arfield
5. No, he came on as a sub
6. True
7. Rangers
8. Celtic
9. Own goal

Odd One Out — P42

1. Glen Kamara (signed from Dundee)

Steven Davis — P42

1. £3m
2. Allan McGregor
3. Southampton
4. None
5. True

Name The Team — P43

1. Joe Aribo
2. Leon Balogun
3. Connor Goldson
4. Calvin Bassey
5. Jon McLaughlin
6. Amad Diallo
7. John Lundstram
8. Steven Davis
9. James Tavernier
10. Scott Arfield
11. Ryan Kent

Brain Buster — P56

1. Five
2. False, Dick Advocaat was the first in 1998
3. Zambia
4. 1997
5. 2015
6. 27
7. Everton
8. True – he scored 355
9. 40
10. Feyenoord

Wordfit — P57

LOVE MATCH?
GET IT DELIVERED EVERY FORTNIGHT!

6 ISSUES FOR JUST £10!*

PACKED EVERY ISSUE WITH...

- ★ Red-hot gear
- ★ News & gossip
- ★ Stats & quizzes
- ★ Massive stars
- ★ Posters & pics
- & loads more!

HOW TO SUBSCRIBE TO MATCH!

CALL 📱
01959 543 747
QUOTE: MATRA23

ONLINE 🖱
SHOP.KELSEY.CO.UK/ MATRA23

ROLL OF HONOUR

EUROPEAN CUP WINNERS' CUP
1971-72

SCOTTISH PREMIERSHIP
1890-91, 1898-99, 1899-1900, 1900-01, 1901-02, 1910-11, 1911-12, 1912-13, 1917-18, 1919-20, 1920-21, 1922-23, 1923-24, 1924-25, 1926-27, 1927-28, 1928-29, 1929-30, 1930-31, 1932-33, 1933-34, 1934-35, 1936-37, 1938-39, 1946-47, 1948-49, 1949-50, 1952-53, 1955-56, 1956-57, 1958-59, 1960-61, 1962-63, 1963-64, 1974-75, 1975-76, 1977-78, 1986-87, 1988-89, 1989-90, 1990-91, 1991-92, 1992-93, 1993-94, 1994-95, 1995-96, 1996-97, 1998-99, 1999-2000, 2002-03, 2004-05, 2008-09, 2009-10, 2010-11, 2020-21

SCOTTISH CHAMPIONSHIP
2015-16

SCOTTISH LEAGUE ONE
2013-14

SCOTTISH LEAGUE TWO
2012-13

SCOTTISH CUP
1893-94, 1896-97, 1897-98, 1902-03, 1927-28, 1929-30, 1931-32, 1933-34, 1934-35, 1935-36, 1947-48, 1948-49, 1949-50, 1952-53, 1959-60, 1961-62, 1962-63, 1963-64, 1965-66, 1972-73, 1975-76, 1977-78, 1978-79, 1980-81, 1991-92, 1992-93, 1995-96, 1998-99, 1999-2000, 2001-02, 2002-03, 2007-08, 2008-09, 2021-22

SCOTTISH LEAGUE CUP
1946-47, 1948-49, 1960-61, 1961-62, 1963-64, 1964-65, 1970-71, 1975-76, 1977-78, 1978-79, 1981-82, 1983-84, 1984-85, 1986-87, 1987-88, 1988-89, 1990-91, 1992-93, 1993-94, 1996-97, 1998-99, 2001-02, 2002-03, 2004-05, 2007-08, 2009-10, 2010-11

SCOTTISH CHALLENGE CUP
2015-16

EMERGENCY WAR LEAGUE
1939-40

EMERGENCY WAR CUP
1939-40

SOUTHERN LEAGUE
1940-41, 1941-42, 1942-43, 1943-44, 1944-45, 1945-46

SOUTHERN LEAGUE CUP
1940-41, 1941-42, 1942-43, 1944-45

GLASGOW LEAGUE
1895-96, 1897-98

GLASGOW CUP
1893, 1894, 1897, 1898, 1900, 1901, 1902, 1911, 1912, 1913, 1914, 1918, 1919, 1922, 1923, 1924, 1925, 1930, 1932, 1933, 1934, 1936, 1937, 1938, 1940, 1942, 1943, 1944, 1945, 1948, 1950, 1954, 1957, 1958, 1960, 1969, 1971, 1975 (shared), 1976, 1979, 1983, 1985, 1986, 1987

VICTORY CUP
1946

SUMMER CUP
1942

GLASGOW MERCHANTS CHARITY CUP
1878-79, 1896-97, 1899-1900, 1903-04, 1905-06, 1906-07, 1908-09, 1910-11, 1918-19, 1921-22, 1922-23, 1924-25, 1927-28, 1928-29, 1929-30, 1930-31, 1931-32, 1932-33, 1933-34, 1938-39, 1939-40, 1940-41, 1941-42, 1943-44, 1944-45, 1945-46, 1946-47, 1947-48, 1950-51, 1954-55, 1956-57, 1959-60